PROPHECY

The woman is out of my Divine Order, because she disobeyed my Word from the beginning of creation. She must return back to her rightful place in the Garden before my Son can return to earth. The woman is coming out of the wilderness seeking power, money and prestige, not knowing it is my presence she seeks. I'm the answer, her womb is trying to birth.

Let this book of prophecy help you to return back to the garden, and walk among the trees with your God!!

"For a small moment have I forsaken thee but with great mercies will I gather thee." Isaiah 54:7

END TIME PROPHECY FOR THE WOMAN

Prophetess Flossie Tindale-Tremble

END TIME PROPHECY FOR THE WOMAN

Prophetess Flossie Tindale-Tremble

OSLP
GPS

Newark, Delaware

Published by Gladstone Publishing Services
Senior Editor: One Smart Lady Productions

For more information:
info@gladstonepublishing.com

Book Cover Photographer:
Ed Correa
EdCorreaPhotography@gmail.com

First Edition

ISBN: 978-1-978681-50-2

Scripture quotations marked KJV are from the Holy Bible, King James Version.

Printed in United States of America

10 9 8 7 6 5 4 3 2 1

Dedication

End Time of Prophecy For The Woman is dedicated to the creation of God's woman. No matter what color creed, nationality or origin; the woman that is bound in a wheelchair, a hospital bed, a convalescent home, a prison, an abused relationship; the woman who is afraid of her own shadow, or stuck in the wilderness, God is calling you. Get up and follow Christ so you can birth what you are carrying in your womb.

Acknowledgement

Thanks! To my late parents, Charlie Tindale and Viola Simon-Tindale, who raised eight children with morals and integrity.

Thanks! To my late husband, John Tremble, Jr., and my daughters, Dawn A. Tremble-Sablo and Jennifer C. Tremble-King, who are the fruit of my womb; and my five grandchildren who are a blessing from God.

Also to the Pastors that ordain me as a Leader in the body of Christ.

Elder

East Side Presbyterian Church
Paterson, New Jersey

Pastor Charles Lindnes

Evangelist

Mount Holiness Temple
Pentecostal Faith Church
Hackensack, New Jersey

Pastor William Moss and
Co-Pastor Jarvis Williamson

Reverend

City of Light/Hunter's
Non-Denominational
Ministries
Houston, Texas

Pastors Charles and Frances
Hunter

My final thanks to Deborah Smart, a great woman of God and my Publisher, who is my friend.

Table of Contents

Dedication.. i

Acknowledgements.. iii

Foreword.. vii

Introduction.. xi

End Time Prophecy for The Woman.......... xv

Chapter One - The Voice of God................ 1

Chapter Two - Confirming His Prophecy
in the Spirit... 14

Chapter Three - God's Written Word......... 21

Chapter Four - September 8, 2001 -
Twin Towers... 24

Chapter Five - Scriptures of Women Who
Carried God's Word.................................. 28

Chapter Six - The Womb is Still
Crying Out... 33

Chapter Seven - God's Prophecy............ 44

Chapter Eight - Conclusion 48

Notes.. 57

Message from the Author........................ 61

Foreword

This book, "The End Time Prophecy for The Woman" is written primarily in the voice of God. Prophetess Tindale-Tremble is releasing the words birthed from her womb. Please understand, this book gives the woman her marching orders. It is time to return to the Garden from the Wilderness where we dwell.

God's Word brings life and purpose to the life of today's woman. As you read this book, take note of how you are highly favored and regarded as the chosen vessel.

Envision a child placed in your womb being nurtured, housed and protected. God's Prophesy has been nurtured, housed and protected for the past 48 years. Prophetess Tindale-Tremble's assignment is being released to you throughout the reading of this book. It is time for the birth of the "End Time Prophecy for The Woman".

The god of this world cannot defeat us. We are no longer under the order of man. God's Word is our protection and shield. Good news, for even the barren woman will give birth to His Word. All women are called back to the Garden. Return to the Garden where it all began and will all end. There is peace in the Garden. God is in the Garden waiting to walk once again with the Woman among the trees.

Hallelujah!

Deborah Smart
Publisher
Biblical Counselor
Woman of God

"Out of Darkness Comes the Light!"

Introduction

The Authoritative Voice of God

"The woman is carrying in her womb my prophecy for End Time. I am visiting the woman with my spirit on every continent throughout the earth.

Now is the time to Release my prophecy to all women on every continent. I demand you to Release what I have put in your mouth (womb). I visited you on February 1969, in a vision. I touched your mouth with my hand and left without a sound. You have been carrying my prophecy in your womb for many, many years. The time has come for you to Release it. You try to figure the vision out without understanding it. You have kept this vision in your spirit and went from church to church for help, but it was not yet time to Release the prophecy. When you didn't know where or what you were doing, you continued to follow me. Through pain, sorrow and disappointed hardship, you did not give up."

The Vision

This prophecy began in 1969, when I had no knowledge and understanding of God's Word. God visited me through His Holy Spirit late one Sunday evening around 4:30 pm, while I was awake lying in my bed. He came in my room kissed the palm of my hand and left without a sound.

He left me a prophecy. He left me a mission that I was not prepared to act on at that time. I kept it inside of me until now.

END TIME PROPHECY
FOR THE WOMAN

"And the woman fled into the wilderness, where she hath a place prepared of God, that should feed her there a thousand two hundred and threescore days."

(Revelation 12:6)

As we read this prophecy; we pray Father that you will guide the footsteps of all women, help them to release your power of truth. Let the truth become alive as you speak through the woman's womb. Lord help the woman to know, without a doubt the gift of Words that she needs to know. Help her to know what she is carrying in her womb, and how to operate in the power of the Holy Spirit. Father, we thank you for the woman who is coming out of the wilderness by the drove that is not really sure on how to release that special gift you have bestowed upon her. Father the woman honors you and your Word, and realizes she needs to return back to the Garden from where she was created and formed into your image. Father, she now has that opened ear to hear your voice and sit at your footstool. We ask this in the name of your Son, the Lord Jesus Christ. Amen

Chapter One

The Voice of God

The will of God is flowing in every area of your body letting you know that His Spirit is residing with you and always will. Seek His Will for your life and He will open up your womb bringing forth His Word. Some of you barren women are still waiting for your womb to carry the baby (Word). Remember what God placed in your womb in the Garden, and what He said to the first woman. He gave her instructions in how she was supposed to carry the baby. God has not changed his Divine Order, on how he is bringing it to pass. Do not give up on God and His Word.

"And the rib, which the Lord had taken from the man, made woman, and brought her unto the man." (Genesis 2:22) This was the creation of God before the fall of man. I'm reminding the woman, the conversation we had before she was presented to her husband. The amazing conversation we had and how she seemed to understand the significance of My Word. The woman was given a womb and every life comes through the gate of her womb.

Woman! Your womb is the enemy's target, you are not what satan is after; do not flatter yourself. His mission is to abort my word and my creation, that you are carrying in your womb. Your womb is the gateway for every life that enters into the Earth. You do not realize it is not about you, it is what you are carrying in your womb. You have abused the womb and become barren. My Spirit grieves whenever a life is ended before it begins. Your womb must return back to the original plan, the beginning of creation starting over using the womb for what I created it to be.

Satan cannot steal God's Word, but he can help destroy the ability for you to believe and understand the truth that is in your womb. After he twisted the truth, you then became defensive trying to defend yourself. From the beginning of creation, he used false doctrines and lies, you should know, you were there, he tricked you. "Yea, Hath God said?" That was all he needed to say, to get you to doubt God's Word, and get you to give up your womb. Those words caused you to fly into the wilderness. "And the woman fled into the wilderness, where she hath a place prepared of God, that they should feed her there a thousand two hundred and threescore days." (Revelations 12:6)

I want the woman to know I have heard her cry for centuries and through all ages. But I cannot go against my own creation and Word. I, myself, must carry out the plan I created. I want you to know that you are released from the wilderness. Your wilderness suffering has come to an end. My Son is waiting on you because my End Time begins with your womb and will end the same way.

The womb is impregnated with God's Word waiting on you to release what you are carrying in your womb. You cannot bring forth His Word through your own strength, you need His love, strength and power to help stop aborting the babies spiritually and naturally. It is restoration time, and God is waiting to restore to you what satan stole from you in the Garden ("Yea, Hath God Said?"). Satan is still tricking the woman today because she is still eating from the forbidden tree ("Yea, Hath God Said?").

My Holy Spirit will impart faith in your heart to remove a mountain of suffering, pain, and sorrow. Your mountain stands, between my Spirit and your spirit, separating you from me. My desire is to bring my Word through your womb and bring life to earth.

Anyone who speaks against my Word and operates out of the lies of man will come to be demised, and will no longer be.

"But the God of all grace, who hath called us unto his eternal glory by Christ Jesus, after that ye have suffered a while, make you perfect, stablish, strengthen, settle you." (1 Peter 5:10)

This prophecy all began in 1969 with a visit from God. He visited me late one Sunday afternoon and left me with a vision I had no knowledge of, and lack of understanding. He kissed my hand and left without a sound. It left me without a clue, but I kept it in my heart for many years. I had never experienced the presence of God in that way before. The vision continued to haunt me until I recognized God was speaking, and God is speaking to you right now.

The Father could have created anything other than a woman, but he loves the woman. Otherwise he would have destroyed her in the Garden in the beginning when lust filled her eyes, and she desired the forbidden fruit. This fruit was sinful to the human race. The deceiver still has the same effect on the woman today as when the first woman sinned.

God gives some of his people the ability to judge the truth. When that happens, you need to be aware of a truth or a lie, and who you're speaking with. Satan wants to destroy the truth that you are carrying in your womb, and change the truth for a lie.

Satan cannot steal God's Word, but he can try to destroy your ability to believe and understand God's Word and the truth that is in your womb. After he twists the truth in your womb, you then become defensive by trying to defend yourself. From the beginning, false misconceptions of God's Word about the woman caused her to flee into the spiritual wilderness.

It is God's Word of power that is within you to create miracles. Don't be afraid of those who do not know the truth, that you were called to bring forth my Word and prophecy. Keep your eyes on your assignment and focus on me your God and the blood of my Son Jesus Christ, and His blood that defeated satan and everything that is around him. Focus and focus.

If you want that relationship with the Father you must go back through your own spiritual womb. You must plant your seeds and give them time for the harvest. Continue to seek to birth the gift God has given to you through His Spirit. Take the mask off and let satan be seen for who he is, a thief, liar, and a destroyer. He is hidden behind the mask.

When you take heed to this prophecy you will begin to travel in space and time in the spirit realm with your Spirit, Soul and Body. With God, there is no time. Whatever happens to the woman, it was told to her from the beginning of creation, but she doubted God's Word. Your time has come and it is right now, receive it.

A man needs a woman to birth his seed. She can help him bring forth the Word because she is the spiritual guide to birthing God's Word into the world. Follow the Word. Don't look for it to follow you. It is God's Divine Order.

Tell them what I have told you. Whether they listen or not my Word has already been created in the spirit realm and it must be done right now in the natural.

Everything you will ever need is in the spirit realm and the Holy Spirit will bring it to you. Ask the Holy Spirit to show you because He is your helpmate. You have to ask the Holy Spirit to help. No one can go in or out, without the help of the Holy Spirit and the woman's womb.

"Speak life over your daughters and let that Word brood and manifest itself." (Dutch Sheet from the book "Intercessory Prayer") Woman proclaim your rightful place back in the Garden, in the presence of God, and God will connect His Spirit back to you. Give up all your ideals for Your Heavenly

Father's Ideals, the mystery of God's Spirit is hidden in His Word.

Speak yourself back into creation, and on how God created the woman. When you think you cannot live without things, that should be a red flag.

The fall of the curse from the first woman will continue with your daughter, until you break that cycle over her. You break that curse with prayer and remind God of His promise He made to you in the Garden.

Satan used the first woman to activate his earthly power. He asked her, "Yea, Have God Said…?" Satan cannot operate without a living flesh, he impregnated the first woman's womb with his seed. That is the reason why he was able to come through the channel of this world. Satan knew he had to be born and the only way was through a woman's womb. That is the reason why he went to her. God allowed this situation to arise in order to let the woman see her mistake. Satan is trying to birth his lies through her womb even now.

God's Word stands no matter what generation fails to obey it. Time has effect on how you approach the Word, but the end result was, and always will be the Word of God and woman.

Woman doesn't give life, she is just the carrier. It is God's creation and He separated light from darkness and brought forth light. God separated the flesh from the spirit of the woman, they are totally different. The Spirit of God is the womb, and the woman is carrying the baby. God requires His creation back to Him from the beginning.

The mother, of our Lord and Savior, Jesus Christ birthed the Word in the flesh, but God ordained the woman to birth the Word in the spirit. The barren woman is not to be wearied. God is waiting on her to birth and deliver His Word through her spiritual womb.

The Father is calling all women back to him. Jesus died and was raised from the dead for her freedom, and only the woman that seek after his righteousness will be used for his glory. If she does not seek to be loose from her burdens and comes out of the wilderness, the woman will die. She will die and never use her womb for the good of creation.

Chapter Two

Confirming His Prophecy
in the Spirit

In 1993, while sitting in the pew of a non-denominational church waiting for the preacher to take his place at the podium, I could hear a voice in my spirit speaking to me and reminding me of the 1969 vision, I kissed your hand with my mouth. "Before I formed thee in the belly I knew thee; and before thou camest forth out of the womb I sanctified thee, and I ordained thee a prophet unto the nations." (Jeremiah 1:5) That was the answer to the vision, and the Holy Spirit was helping me to remember and understand.

He said, "now that you have a little more knowledge of my Word, you must continue to build upon it and trust me to bring it to pass. I thought I was ready to take on the world, but the Holy Spirit reminded me that my journey had just begun. "There will be ups and downs before my Word can be fulfilled in your womb." I thought I needed man to validate me, but the Holy Spirit reminded me that God himself validated and promoted his chosen. I am writing this prophecy from His hand and what He has placed in my mouth, and the prophecy entered my womb.

Recently, I had a visit from a woman while sitting by my sister's hospital bed waiting for God's healing power to restore her health. After the prayers had gone up before the Lord, and the Doctor's skills and experiences were at work, the only thing we could do was to continue to pray and trust God would bring her through. This woman walked into the room and stopped short of coming to me and said, "You're a Prophet! There are some that would oppose, try and stop you, but you continue to do what God called you to do."

I questioned her on who she was, but she had no answer for me and no one seemed to know where she came from. After she left, an inward voice reminded me of what took place over the many years of the visions and dreams God had shown me through my spirit. I then understood and realized that my time had come for me to know when God is speaking, and what He is revealing to me for His End Time.

God spoke to me and said the following.

"I want woman to know that I have heard her cry for centuries and throughout all ages. I couldn't go against my own Word. I, myself, must carry out the plan I created. I want you to know that you are released from the wilderness. Your wilderness suffering has come to an end. My Son is waiting on you, because End Time begins with you and your womb, and will end the same way, with the Word.

This book of prophecy started with my Word and creation in the Garden; and has not changed. It will live throughout eternity. I want you to know, understand and to realize that every life that enters into the world comes through a woman's womb.

That is my Divine Order and that can never change."

The Word of life comes through the gateway of a woman's Spiritual womb

The woman has been carrying my word in the womb for many years without understanding. Now I speak and remind you, of the conversation we had in the garden, to connect you back to me. Your womb is barren, shut up and destroyed for lack of wisdom, knowledge and understanding. You're still eating the fruit from the forbidden tree, trying to find pleasure, happiness and gain from the world. Judgment follows the disobedience of My Word and will end at eternity. The world belongs to me and will bow to every word I speak before my Son comes back to earth.

The god of this world blankets your mind with pain, sorrow, suffering and hardship that keeps you in the wilderness and continues to hold you back. My Son came in the form of flesh and manifest himself in My Word. When Mary, the natural mother of my Son Jesus Christ realized her purpose and the assignment I had given to her to do, "She said, Behold the handmaid of the Lord; be it unto me according to thy Word. And the angel departed from her." (St. Luke 1:38) Woman, this is your time and season to combat any battle that holds you back from hearing my voice and stopping you from carrying out the assignment I have given to you. My Son Jesus went down into hell and loose everything that would hold you back and stop My Word from coming through your womb. My Word has been distorted, misplaced and manipulated by the system of this world.

The spiritual gravity of my world is changing back to the beginning of creation with the woman who is the carrier. Your time has come to release the purity of My Word and bring back the purity of my sons and daughters that I created in your womb and in my image for my glory.

As I speak to you, listen for my voice to guide, direct and bring back what I place in your womb from the beginning of my creation. My Holy Spirit is waiting on you to open the gateway of your spiritual womb and to allow me to bring forth My Word.

Chapter Three

God's Written Word

I am revealing this prophecy to the woman and the life she is carrying in her womb. End Time will begin with the beginning of creation. I designed the woman for a special purpose for birthing My Word (babies). She has been given that special assignment. The world might say focus not on the past, it is behind us and we cannot return back. The present is a reflection of the past and future, always representing the beginning of the present, because creation never changes. Changes began in the Garden with man when I created them. "And the rib, which the Lord God had taken from the man, made woman, and brought her unto the man." (Genesis 2:22) You had been falling in darkness until my Son came to earth.

Everyone is looking for my Son to return to earth for End Time. Let me assure you that he cannot until Divine Order has been replaced and restored. From the beginning of time, the enemy tried to change my Word of prophecy that came through my chosen vessels.

I am restoring the woman's relationship back to me for my glory. I gave the woman special instructions at the beginning of her creation, and my decision was not created by man's thinking. Everything is placed in Divine Order and cannot be changed. I, myself, must honor my Word. My Spirit

(Word) had to be protected by the womb of the woman and she is the carrier.

This prophecy and assignment was placed in the womb of a woman in 1969. Now the time has come for her to remind the woman that she is free and no longer under the thinking of man. Her time has come to birth my Word on every continent and not be afraid of the enemy, my Son, Jesus Christ paid it all at the Cross.

Chapter Four

September 8, 2001-
Twin Towers

As I reflect back on a September 8th 2001 dream where I saw the Twin Towers, in New York, brought down to the ground and destroyed. I realize I was not mature in the Word of God and had no understanding of His presence in my life. When the Twin Towers came down on September 11, 2001, on my own, I tried to make sense out of what was going on with this dream of prophecy. After being affected by the many people who died that day, I was left with a burden that haunted me for a long time.

I asked myself over and over, if I had the courage to tell and/or say what God had revealed to me at that time, "What would have happened?" After a long period of time God revealed to me, "this judgement was not to be told by you. I wanted you to understand and recognize this was for you.

"I have placed prophecy in your womb and at the right season you will release it to the people," said your God. "I am releasing my judgment on earth as a warning for the people to see and feel the power of my wrath, because they have disobeyed my Word."

Now, I do understand and have knowledge of the maturity of God's Word, and how you must apply it at God's timing. Prophecy comes with maturity, and with age, and having a personal relationship with the Father.

Woman! God is speaking to you so very loud and you cannot hear him, because you have shut up your spiritual and physical womb. Your womb was created to release the very nature of God into the earth. The long time in the wilderness is over, and God is bringing you out and no one can stop the hand of God.

"Woman died a spiritual death in the Garden. It was very painful, and brought sorrow to the woman and she had to endure hardship from the beginning of creation. I am releasing you to spread my Word to every nation. You are stopping my Son from returning back to earth. You are part of my Divine Order. Listen and hear the Prophetess and live for eternity. My creation plan has not changed and my Word was put in force by my Spirit and cannot be changed by nothing or no one."

God instructed me:

"The sound of your voice will be my voice, and I will echo through your voice and the woman and man will be transformed. There is a significant meaning in every step you take. The power of darkness is destroyed. You need to proclaim what is yours and take back your heavenly place with me.

I will confirm what is written in this book not anyone else nor can anyone stand against my Word and my woman of God."

Chapter Five

Scriptures of Women Who Carried God's Word

These are scriptures of women who have carried God's Word in their Womb.

"NOW THE serpent was more subtle than any beast of the field which the Lord God had made. And he said unto the woman, "Yea, hath God said? Ye shall not eat of every tree of the Garden?" (Genesis 3:1) The serpent knew the woman was carrying the answer to his question in her womb that is the reason he went to her. He wanted to know which tree had the sin of death, so that he could come through and cause men to obey him.

The woman said to him; "But the fruit of the tree which is in the midst of the Garden, God hath said. Ye shall not eat of it, neither shall ye touch it, lest ye die." (Genesis 3:3) That is when he impregnated her womb and he had his answer.

"And behold thou shall conceive in thy womb, and bring forth a son, and shalt call his name JESUS (The Word)." (St. Luke 1:31) Mary (womb), became the mother of our Lord and Savior Jesus Christ.

"And, it came to pass, that when Elizabeth (womb) heard the salutation of Mary, the baby leaped in her womb; and Elizabeth was filled with the Holy Ghost." (St. Luke

1:41) Elizabeth (womb), became the mother of John the Baptist, the forerunner before Jesus Christ.

"And she (Elizabeth) spake out with a loud voice, and said, Blessed art thou among women, and blessed is the fruit of thy womb." (St. Luke 1:42)

"Jesus saith unto her (Mary Magdalene), Woman (womb) why weepest thou? Whom seekest thou?" (St. John 20:15)

"Jesus saith unto her, Mary. She turned herself and saith unto him, Rabboni which is to say Master." (St. John 20:16)

"Jesus saith unto her, Touch me not, for I am not yet ascended to my Father: but go to my brethren, and say unto them, I ascend unto my Father, and your Father; and to my God, and your God." (St. John 20:17)

Mary Magdalene (womb) was the first person to talk with Jesus Christ after his death, burial and resurrection. He gave her the word, and she carried it in her womb, and gave it to the others.

The Samaritan woman (womb) "then left her waterpot, and went her way into the city, and saith to the men, Come, see a man which told me all things that ever I did: is not this the Christ?" (St. John 4:28-29) She was carrying the word in her womb to the people. These women were all carriers just like you and I today.

You can be successful in your own strength, but your strength will not help you with the gateway of your womb to bring your sons and daughters with my power and strength into the earth.

Chapter Six

The Womb is Still Crying Out Today

When Hillary Clinton ran for President of United States, she had to go through a fire of hate, lies, and resentment.

The enemy saw the greatness I placed in Hillary Clinton's womb and he tried to abort it by tearing her character down with lies. While millions of people disliked her, millions of people did. They understood that she was called to stand in the gap for all women. The enemy tried to abort my Word I created in her womb. She understands the power that was given to her by my Spirit.

She broke that glass ceiling and provided a path for all women to follow her footsteps by obeying the God-given gifts I have created in her womb. Hillary was abused, battered and shattered, because I chose her to carry my Word and purpose. She endured pain, sorrow and hardship for carrying her assignment that was given by me that I created in her womb.

There had been times she wanted to give up, but she understood the greatness of my power. She might not have had the know how to go about her assignment, because the path was not spelled out for her to know exactly what she is carrying in her womb. Nevertheless, she follows the path I chose for her. Remember the fight is between the woman and satan, and not the man.

Remember what took place in the Garden
and what I allowed satan to hear. That's the
reason he first went to the woman, to trick
her to release what was in her womb. He is
still seeking to destroy the babies that have
the Word. He understands that End Time
begins with him and will end with him.
Everything will be returned back to me. He
cannot accept that you have the power that
will destroy him for End Time and forever.
Amen

I want the woman to know that the curse
is broken from over her life, and she
is redeemed from the curse of the law,
redeemed from sickness and redeemed
from poverty, and redeemed from death.
My Son paid it all at the cross.

Woman you cannot abort what is in your womb, the babies, dreams, visions and the ability to bring life into the earth. It is one of the greatest gifts God could have ever bestowed upon the woman. Your womb is the carrier, and your womb has been shut up not allowing the power of God to come through you. You are free, and whom God's Son set free is free indeed.

God wants to release the power He has given to you for His glory.

The United States might have learned from 1 Samuel 8:6. The people wanted a king and they disrespected the Word, and lived without principles and guidelines. Saul led the people to disobey the Word of God.

November 2016, the United States voted a President into office knowing his viewpoint, and how he viewed the womb of a woman. His viewpoint about the woman is not of God, because he himself came through a woman's womb. Every life must come to earth through a woman's womb.

The forefathers of this country put in a law that would protect all the citizens of the United States. The Constitution was written and implemented with principles and guidelines for the people to follow. This was God's Divine Order for his children. Many Christians supported and voted this person into office knowing his viewpoint and how he viewed God's creation.

His platform is making "America Great Again."
America is already great with materialistic things,
but has lost the way to eternity.

God's Word to me said:

"Man has entered into a dark place with
greed, lies and immorality. I separated the
light from darkness so that man can become
that light and share my glory. 'And God saw
the light, that it was good and God divided
the light from the darkness.' (Genesis 1:4) I
want man to shine that light in dark places."

God wants man to know that there is only
one of each kind I created in the garden.
"So, God created man in his own image,
in the image of God created he him, male
and female created he them." (Genesis

1:27) I am shifting my creation back into my original plan that was created from the beginning.

From the beginning, man followed self-righteousness, self-accomplishment and self-greed. The people followed the thinking of man and shifted out of the realm of My Word and the people were led to do evil work. The people have disregarded My Word, disarmed My truth and dismantled their thinking. He sees good through his own eyes and will do whatever feels good. There is an evil voice going out into my universe leading man to his demise.

Many of my people are falling away from the church. The enemy has tried to sabotage My Word and destroy My Creation.

The woman's womb is still satan's focus. The woman is carrying what he desires to destroy, that is My Word. The woman has the answer in her womb for End Time.

The strange voice that your children are hearing is that of satan. That voice is going into the world, and blankets the mind of our children. It has over shadowed my World with lies, greed and immorality. Before the babies come out of the womb, they are confronted with hearing the wrong voices.

God revealed to me that your child has a common enemy and his name is satan. You cannot see him with your natural eyes, but God sees him for you and your child. Satan is still attacking your womb and killing your child. The womb is being attacked, and the child are being destroyed in it. Killing a child is the norm for the enemy, because he is after the creation of My Word, "Yea hath God said."

A mother is mourning the death of her child, because of the lies, greed and immorality that have penetrated in the heart and soul of man. Killing have always been satan's target for destroying My Word, but I have given the woman my power and strength to stop the killing that is taken place in her womb.

God is saying to the woman, it is time to wake up! Look to me and let me help you understand what is happening to your son and daughter, this all began in my garden. "Yea hath God said."

There is a cry in the woman's womb going out all over the world with a heartfelt need for help! A woman's womb needs to be protected by the blood and Word of Jesus Christ. God is waiting on you woman to return back to Him in the garden, where He gave life, and where it all began with the man and woman. Satan is still attacking the womb even now as this Prophecy is being written by a chosen vessel.

You have changed the truth of My Word for gain and preached Jesus is coming soon, but are not preaching what I have commanded you to preach.

My people are falling away from the church because the enemy has sabotaged My Word with lies, greed and immorality. The Word has become non-effective in the church and the lives of the people. They have turned the truth of My Word for gain.

From the beginning of creation man has allowed the enemy to sift them like wheat. The truth is unfolding with signs and wonders for End Time. The woman's womb is still satan's focus. The woman is carrying what he desires, to destroy. My Word! The woman has the answer in her womb.

Our children should be listening to the voice of God. Some of the people are only preaching Jesus Christ is coming soon, and we are at the door of End Time. What our children should be listening to is (Roman 6:23) "For the wages of sin is death; but the gift of God is eternal life through Jesus Christ our Lord."

Chapter Seven

God's Prophecy

October 10, 2010, God said, "I am sending you to Lima Peru to prophesize My Word. Tell the people I have heard their prayers, and I am restoring what the enemy has stolen. It is restoration time for the people to receive the blessing that is already theirs. You have planted your seed and the time for your harvest is right now."

I made plans to fly to Lima Peru. I needed help because I didn't speak their language. The Holy Spirit reminded me that God honors His Word and I need not be concerned. "The interpreter was already walking alongside me. Eusebia E. Heckle is in your midst and has been assigned and chosen to go with you." She was born and raised in that country, so she knew the language.

We made plans to fly to Lima Peru because God was speaking and we wanted to obey His Word. The flight was ten hours and we ran into a storm across the Pacific Ocean. I heard that voice in my spirit again, and it said, "I am with you. Tell my people what I have said and have faith in me to do what I said I would do."

We stayed for ten days and out of those, we ministered seven times. Many people were saved and came to know Jesus Christ for the very first time.

While we were in Lima Peru, we were taken up one of the highest mountains. Pastor O'Rios took us up to visit one of his churches that sits on a high mountain overlooking land and cities. Pastor O'Rios said we're the first clergy to visit the church, others had tried and failed because of the height. Pastor O'Rios said it was always his vision to build a church on that mountain. Others failed to see the vision he was trying to show them. He wanted us to pray with them and thank God for the work they were about to do. While kneeling and worshipping the Lord, I could hear the Spirit of God telling me, the mountain experience is a place I needed to come and worship him. The mountain was placed there for me to be the first Prophetess to look down and see His Spirit as He moved throughout the land seeing His prophecy come to pass.

God is restoring back to the people what was lost in time and space. God is going to restore what the enemy had stolen from them because God heard their prayers and their cries have come up to Him. Eusebia and I were chosen to bring the good news to His people and to prophesize His Word.

At that moment we knew God brought us there to test our faith and demonstrate His power that was within our womb. We kneeled and worshipped. We knew He brought us there for His Divine Purpose. He allowed us to be the first clergy or missionary to visit that mountain. We didn't take it for granted that this was something very special and connected to our spirit. This memory is still with me and I will continue to follow my dreams, visions, the encounter with the Holy Spirit and that special visit to Peru.

Chapter Eight

Conclusion

Isaiah 54:1-8; 10; 13-17

1 SING, O barren, thou that didst not bear; break forth into singing, and cry aloud, thou that didst not travail with child; for more are the children of the desolate than the children of the married wife, saith the Lord.

2 Enlarge the place of thy tent, and; let them stretch forth the curtains of thine habitations: spare not,

lengthen thy cords, and strengthen thy stakes;

3 For thou shalt break forth on the right hand and on the left; and thy seed shall inherit the Gentiles and make the desolate cities to be inhabited.

4 Fear not; for thou shalt not be ashamed; neither be thou confounded; for thou shalt not be put to shame: for thou shalt forget the shame of thy youth, and shalt not remember the reproach of thy widowhood any more.

5 For thy Maker is thine husband; the Lord of hosts is his name; and

thy Redeemer the Holy One of Israel; The God of the whole earth shall he be called.

6 For the Lord hath called thee as a woman forsaken and grieved in spirit, and a wife of youth, when thou wast refused, saith thy God.

7 For a small moment have I forsaken thee; but with great mercies will I gather thee.

8 In a little wrath I hid my face from thee for a moment; but with everlasting kindness will I have mercy in thee, saith the Lord thy Redeemer.

10 For the mountain shall depart, and the hills be removed; but my kindness shall not depart from thee, neither shall the covenant of my peace be removed, saith the Lord that hath mercy on thee.

13 And all thy children shall be taught of the Lord; and great shall be the peace of their children.

14 In righteousness shalt thou be established: thou shalt thou be far from oppression; for thou shalt not fear: and from terror; for it shall not come near thee.

15 Behold, they shall surely gather together, but not by me: whosoever

shall gather together against thee shall fall for my sake.

17 No weapon that is formed against thee shall prosper; and every tongue that shall rise against thee in judgment thou shalt condemn. This is the heritage of the servants of the Lord, and their righteousness is of me, saith the Lord...Amen

God wants man to know that there is only one of each kind He created in the Garden. "So, God created man in his own image, in the image of God created he him; male and female created he them." (Genesis 1:27) I am shifting my creation back into my original plan that was created from the beginning.

Conclusion

Get ready for the last battle (death). "So, when this corruptible shall have put on incorruption, and this mortal shall have put on immortality, then shall be brought to pass the saying that is written, Death is swallowed up in victory." (1 Corinthians 15:54)

End Time Prophecy for The Woman

Conclusion

The Holy Spirit will lead the Woman back to the Garden.

End Time Prophecy for The Woman

NOTES

Message from the Author

Prophetess Flossie Tindale-Tremble

I was diagnosed with fibrosis cyst in my left breast, and had not been sick, or had an overnight stay in a hospital. My Doctor recommended I get it removed. I had no idea what they would find and what was going to happen. They removed the cyst and everything was fine. I was not yet a follower of Jesus Christ and had no understanding of His Word. Yet, His Spirit was with me and I got through it, and all was well. At the time in my life, I experienced the healing blood and power of Jesus Christ.

I decided to go back to school where I attended Felician College in Lodi New Jersey majoring in Religious Studies. It was a two-year program. I also attended New York School of the Bible extended courses in their Old and New Testament Program out of Clifton New Jersey, and City of Light/Hunter Ministries Training Classes in Houston Texas.

You can contact Prophetess Tindale-Tremble at the following address:

Healing House Ministry, Inc.
P.O. Box 12012
Wilmington, DE 19850

www.ingramcontent.com/pod-product-compliance
Lightning Source LLC
Chambersburg PA
CBHW070831100426
42813CB00003B/580